THE POCKET
Pickleball

Published in 2025
by Gemini Books
Part of Gemini Books Group

Based in Woodbridge and London

Marine House, Tide Mill Way,
Woodbridge, Suffolk IP12 1AP
United Kingdom

www.geminibooks.com

Part of the Gemini Pockets series

Cover illustration: Shutterstock/sportoakimirka

ISBN 978-1-80247-285-1

A CIP catalogue record for this book is available from the British Library.

Printed in China

10 9 8 7 6 5 4 3 2 1

Shutterstock: 3 / sportoakimirka; 7 / DGTL Graphics sro; 8, 22, 23, 46, 51, 52, 69, 74, 86 / Tani Kuzminka. Adobe Stock: 12, 44, 88, 91, 92, 93, 94, 95, 101, 110, 111, 113, 114, 116, 117, 119–127 / sljubisa; 39 / Silard; 52 / BestNerdLife; 57 / Richard O'Donoghue; 70, 73 / sinemaslow; 206 / Tani Kuzminka. Vecteezy: 66, 102 / kinggod.

THE POCKET

Pickleball

G:

Contents

Introduction

It doesn't matter if you've yet to pick up a paddle – we bet you've heard of pickleball. The sport is everywhere, and not just because of its memorable name.

People across the globe are taking up pickleball as their hobby of choice, and they're doing so in droves. In the United States alone, *millions* of people play the sport. And other countries are following suit – from Samoa to the United Arab Emirates, from Cameroon to Colombia, and nearly everywhere else in between.

This little book – like your local pickleball league – has something for everyone. Newbies can learn the rules, intermediate players can pick up strategy, and pickleball pros can discover which celebrity picklers to look for at their next tournament. So, read on – and then head to the court to put your pickleball prowess to the test.

Chapter One

Pickleball 101

"Everyone from the super young to the super old can take part. It takes minutes to learn the basics, games are short, and all you need is a net, paddle, and ball to get started. It doesn't take much skill to hit the ball, either, because it doesn't move as fast as a tennis ball. The best thing about pickleball, however, is that it's just super fun!"

Bill Gates, Gatesnotes.com, 26 July 2020

Welcome to Pickleball

Let's jump straight in. You've picked up this book with the intention of understanding just *how* the sport of pickleball works.

Of course, the best way to learn is by doing, but getting to know the rules is a good place to start.

Here, we'll cover everything you need to know about the game, from equipment and etiquette, to scoring and strategy.

Pickleball players are known as "picklers".

Tennis vs Badminton vs Ping Pong

Pickleball is often described as a mash-up of tennis, badminton and ping pong, having started life on a badminton court with ping pong rackets (more of that in Chapter Two). Nowadays, a pickleball court is slightly wider and shorter than its shuttlecocking relative, and the paddles are more rectangular than the table-based game.

Players use a paddle to bat a plastic ball over the net. For the first two shots, the ball *must* bounce. Then you can volley to your heart's content.

Read on to find out how service changes hands, how only the serving side can score points, and why you must stay out of the kitchen!

Getting to Know the Court

A pickleball court measures 44 ft (13.4 m) by 20 ft (6.1 m).

The net is 3 ft (91 cm) high.

The court is divided down the middle, into left and right sides – and there is a 7-ft (2.1-m) area each side of the net, known as the non-volley zone – or kitchen.

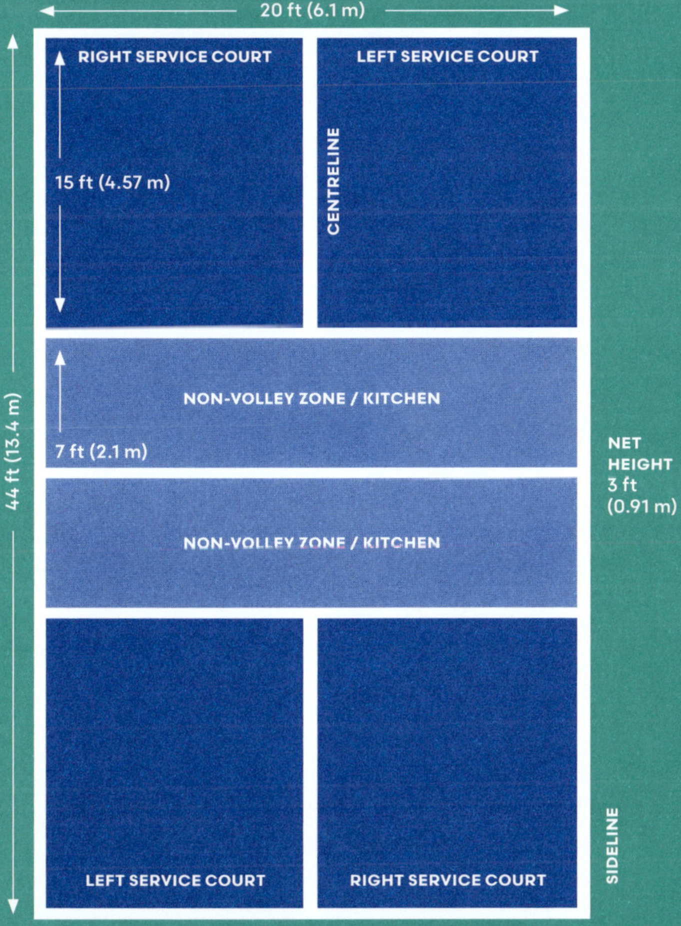
20 ft (6.1 m)
44 ft (13.4 m)
RIGHT SERVICE COURT
LEFT SERVICE COURT
15 ft (4.57 m)
CENTRELINE
NON-VOLLEY ZONE / KITCHEN
7 ft (2.1 m)
NET HEIGHT 3 ft (0.91 m)
NON-VOLLEY ZONE / KITCHEN
LEFT SERVICE COURT
RIGHT SERVICE COURT
SIDELINE

What You'll Need

A paddle

A pickleball paddle (or racket) is squarish in shape, with rounded corners – bigger than a ping pong paddle; smaller than a tennis racket. See page 38 for more on choosing the size and material of your paddle.

Pickleballs

Pickleballs are hollow, perforated plastic balls, slightly larger than tennis balls.

The number of holes vary: indoor pickleballs have 26 holes, while the outdoor version has 40, as it's designed to withstand windy conditions!

A pickleball might last around five games before it loses its bounce (depending on how hard it's hit!).

A court

Pickleball courts are popping up everywhere – at recreation centres and in local public parks, as well as private clubs.

What You Should Wear

Comfy and/or stretchy tops and bottoms
Anything you can easily move around in!

The right trainers
Normal running, walking or cross-training shoes won't cut it on the pickleball court, as they're not designed to support the side-to-side or sliding movements you'll need to succeed in pickleball. Instead, seek out court shoes, which have the perfect amount of grip and ample ankle support for all your pickleball positions.

Sunglasses and/or a cap/visor
If you play outdoors, you'll want to wear a cap, sunglasses or both, in order to keep your visibility – and swing accuracy – as high as possible.

Pickleballs travel at one-third of the speed of tennis balls, due to the holes.

Set Up the Serve

The first thing you'll need to learn is how to serve the ball.

The serving player, whether playing singles or doubles, must serve from the right-hand side of their half of the court, with both feet behind the back line.

There are no overhead, high-speed slams like you see in tennis – pickleball serves can *only* be made underhand.

The ball then must sail diagonally over the net and bounce in the opposite-side box before it is considered to be in play.

How to Serve

- Serves must always be underhand with the paddle below the wrist and below the waist.
- Serve the ball from the air (no bounce) or use a drop serve (releasing the ball from above the paddle, letting it bounce once then hitting it).
- You can serve forehand or backhand.

The option of the drop serve was introduced into pickleball rules in 2021.

Stay Out of "the Kitchen"

On the pickleball court, the 7-ft (2.1-m) rectangle at the front of the court on either side of the net is called the kitchen.

Serves **cannot** bounce in here. They must bounce *past* the kitchen area in order to be in play.

If the ball bounces in the kitchen, it is known as a short serve.

You Only Get One Chance!

You read that right: you only get one chance to get your serve right in pickleball! (This isn't tennis, you know.)

So, remember that it has to be an underhand serve, it has to cross-cut the court, and it can't land in the kitchen!

Let Serves Count

Unlike tennis, if your ball clips the net but still bounces in the correct place, the serve is good.

Up until 2021, let serves were replayed.

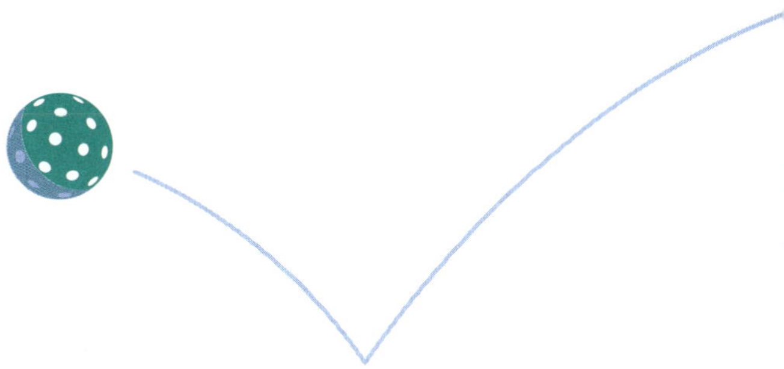

Master the Bounce

Bouncing the ball is very important in pickleball.

A serve has to bounce in the other half before it's in play.

The same goes for the return of the serve – that has to bounce once before it can be paddled back, too.

But unlike a serve, the return can land anywhere on the opponent's side of pickleball court, including in the kitchen!

Third Time Lucky

Once you've both served and returned successfully, the fun really starts.

The third time over the net, a player can return – or volley – the pickleball before it has a chance to bounce.

BUT beware! You cannot volley the ball if you are standing in the kitchen.

You don't have to volley it – you are allowed to let it bounce before returning a winner!

The Momentum Rule

Again, we implore you: stay out of the kitchen!

You're aware that your feet must be out of the kitchen when volleying – but watch out. The momentum rule in pickleball states that, until you finish the motion of a volley and then regain your balance, nothing on your person can breach the boundary of the kitchen.

So, if after you have played the shot and *before* you are solidly back on your feet, if any clothing, hat, paddle or other body part touches the non-volley zone, you will lose the point.

This even applies if your sweat towel happens to fall into the kitchen while you take your shot, or if you bump into your partner and *they* fall in while you volley!

First to 11

Most pickleball games are played to 11 points, and the winning player/team must win by at least 2 points.

That means that if the score's 10–10, and then goes to 11–10, it doesn't end there... The person with 11 points will have to score 1 more, to end on 12–10 (or the player with 10 will have to go for 3 in a row!).

A match will usually consist of the best 2 out of 3 games to 11 points.

Professional tournament games are often played to 11, but they can also be played to 15 or even 21 points.

So, How Do I Score Points?

Only the serving player/team can score points, and they can only do so when the **opposing** player/team makes a fault – see opposite.

When the server has scored a point, they move to the other side of the court for their next shot. So, if they score a point from the right-hand side, their next serve will come from the left-hand side of their side of the court, and so on.

The serving team continues to serve until they do not win a point (and until they themselves fault).

What Is a Fault?

Faults are also known as errors or mistakes. If an opposing player makes one when you or your team have just served, then you get a point.

Examples of faults include:

- **Hitting the ball into the net**
- **Missing a serve return**
- **Allowing the ball to bounce more than once**
- **Hitting the ball out of bounds**
- **Being hit by the ball**
- **Volleying the service ball without letting it bounce**

Remember, it's the non-serving team that must make a fault in order for the server to get a point.

When a ball hits the outer line of the court, it's "in" – unlike in squash when a ball hitting a line would be "out".

How Does the Server Change Over?

If the serving player scores a point, they continue to serve until they make a fault. They continue to swap from the right to left side of the court on each serve.

This means that you will often be serving on the right for odd points, and left for even points.

In **singles**, a server fault means the ball goes to the opposing player.

In **doubles**, both players on the same side get a chance to serve – once they *both* fault, the opposing team takes over!

When the other player on a team takes over serve, they serve from the side on which they are already standing, so the left-right, odd-even pattern may not always be there in doubles!

Share the Score

Before every serve, picklers *must* announce the score.

In singles matches, you must say two numbers: your score first, followed by your opponent's score.

In doubles, servers must say three numbers: your score, your opponents' score, and then the number server you are – 1 or 2. This might look like: 7–4–2.

(If you don't call the score, it doesn't count as a fault – but you must call it before the next rally.)

"My pickleball motto is 'Rip, Bang, Win, Cake!' Rip the ball, bang the ball, win the match, and celebrate with cake!"

Anna Leigh Waters, pro pickleball player, newwestpickleball.com, 2024

Wheelchair Pickleball

In wheelchair pickleball, the ball is allowed to bounce twice before being hit; a third bounce is a fault.

In terms of the kitchen, the smaller front wheels of the pickler's chair can be in the non-volley zone when a volley is played. If the back wheels touch the kitchen area, it is a fault.

Pickleball's rules apply equally to men and women, but they don't play against each other (in tournaments).

Pickleball games are either singles or doubles by gender, or mixed doubles.

Statistically speaking, there are likely to be more gentlemen's matches than ladies' – 67 per cent of pickleballers are male, and the remaining 33 per cent are women.

Choosing the Perfect Paddle: Size

Paddles come in three different sizes:

Standard
The classic paddle size is between 7–8 in (17.8–20.3 cm) wide and 15–16 in (38.1–40.6 cm) long. This suits players of all skill levels, and provides a great balance of reach, power and manoeuvrability.

Elongated
As the name implies, this paddle type is slightly longer than the standard paddle – 16–17 inches (40.6–43.2cm) long – but it's a bit narrower at 6–7 in (15.2–17.8 cm) wide. This gives players a longer reach and more power with their swings; it also makes it easier to chop the ball and create spin. However, an elongated paddle has a smaller sweet spot – the area where you can most powerfully and accurately hit the ball. Pickleball pros recommend this style for those who play singles.

Wide-body

The wide-body paddle is ideal for newbies. Measuring in at 8 in (20.3 cm) wide and 16 in (40.6 cm) long, this paddle has a generous sweet spot. A wide-body paddle is also easy to manoeuvre. However, it may not deliver as much power as an elongated paddle.

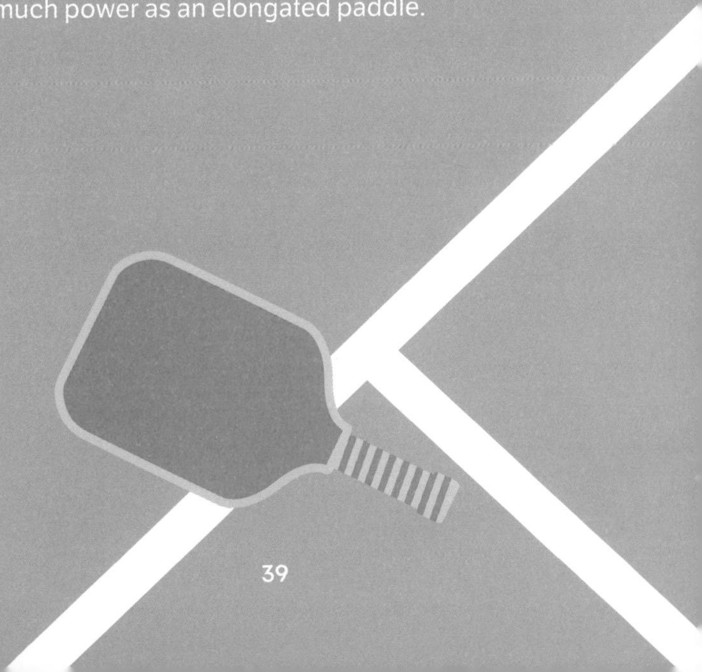

The pickleball paddle market was estimated to be worth $148.5 million (£116 million) in 2021.

It is predicted that by 2028, this will have grown to $254 million (£198 million).

Choosing the Perfect Paddle: Material

The material of the face of your paddle is important – it determines the trajectory, velocity and power of your shot.

Composite
Composite paddles typically provide a good amount of power and spin, and suit picklers of all skill levels. Plus, they're average weight – neither too light nor too heavy.

Nowadays, most pickleball paddles are composite, meaning they're made up of a mixture of at least two of the materials overleaf.

Graphite

There's a reason why graphite is so popular among pickleball players, both casual and professional. It's lightweight, but gives a great amount of power and control.

Fibreglass

This is the most powerful pickleball paddle material; it also comes with a slight texture to provide grip for spinning your shots.

Aluminium

This one's great for beginners – it's lightweight and inexpensive, great for learning the ins and outs of the game!

Carbon fibre

Paddles made from this material give players power and control, and it creates a generous sweet spot, all in a mid-weight paddle.

A heavier paddle creates more power from your shots.

A lighter paddle is easier to manoeuvre and re-position, making it simpler to re-group between shots.

What Else Can I Do to Win?

Knowing the basic rules of pickleball may be enough to help you win.

But a little bit of strategy goes a long way in helping you to become a better pickleball player.

Pickleball Strategy #1

Stand at Attention

You'll be surprised to see how fast a pickleball game can move. Once you are on the court, you'll understand the importance of standing in a ready-to-play stance so you're able to return whatever comes your way.

To get in the "ready" position:

- **Stand facing the net, with your feet shoulder-width apart.**
- **Bend your knees, and try putting your weight on the balls of your feet so you can easily spring toward the ball.**
- **Face your paddle forward or at a slight angle with the head upright.**

Pickleball Strategy #2

Master Your Serve

Remember, you only get one chance to get your serve right before the other player or team gets the ball.

So, spend time getting that underhand move mastered, and your score will greatly improve.

Pickleball Strategy #3

Perfect a Strategic Serve

Once you get comfortable with hitting a returnable serve, you can then work on making your serve bounce within the lines *and* difficult for the opposing player to hit back!

For example, hitting toward the back corner will make for a long return, and some players struggle to return these distance shots.

Pickleball Strategy #4

Return Deep

Hitting the pickleball deep into the back court when you're returning a serve is a great strategy.

Remember that by the *third* shot of the game, the serving team no longer has to bounce the ball, so they will probably try to drive it hard back to you – and that's a very tricky hit to return.

So, stop them in their tracks with a well-placed ball!

Pickleball Strategy #5

Pay Attention to Ball Height

An easy way to win a point – or win the ball back from the opposing side – is to let a ball that's heading out of bounds *go* out of bounds.

That may sound simplistic, but in practice, it's often hard to tell whether a speedy pickleball is going to land out of bounds or just hit the line.

One method is to watch a ball's height as it comes your way. Anything at chest or shoulder height will probably be too high to land in bounds, so just hop out of the way!

Pickleball Strategy #6

Talk to Your Partner

Another way to know when a shot is going out of bounds is to have your doubles partner shout to you that it's headed that way. And that trick brings us to our next major pickleball strategy – communicate with your partner!

This doesn't just help with balls heading out of bounds. When you communicate with your pickleball partner, you can…

- **Share quick strategy tips**
- **Say you've got the ball to avoid a collision**
- **Encourage them during a tough match (and vice versa)**

Pickleball Strategy #7

Don't Second-guess Yourself!

One of the biggest mistakes you can make on the pickleball court is second-guessing yourself. Hesitating for just a few seconds can be the difference between a powerful hit that wins you a point, and missing a playable ball.

So, listen to your instinct, and go with it – it's better to wholeheartedly take an imperfect shot than half-heartedly fire off an attempt at a strategically sound shot.

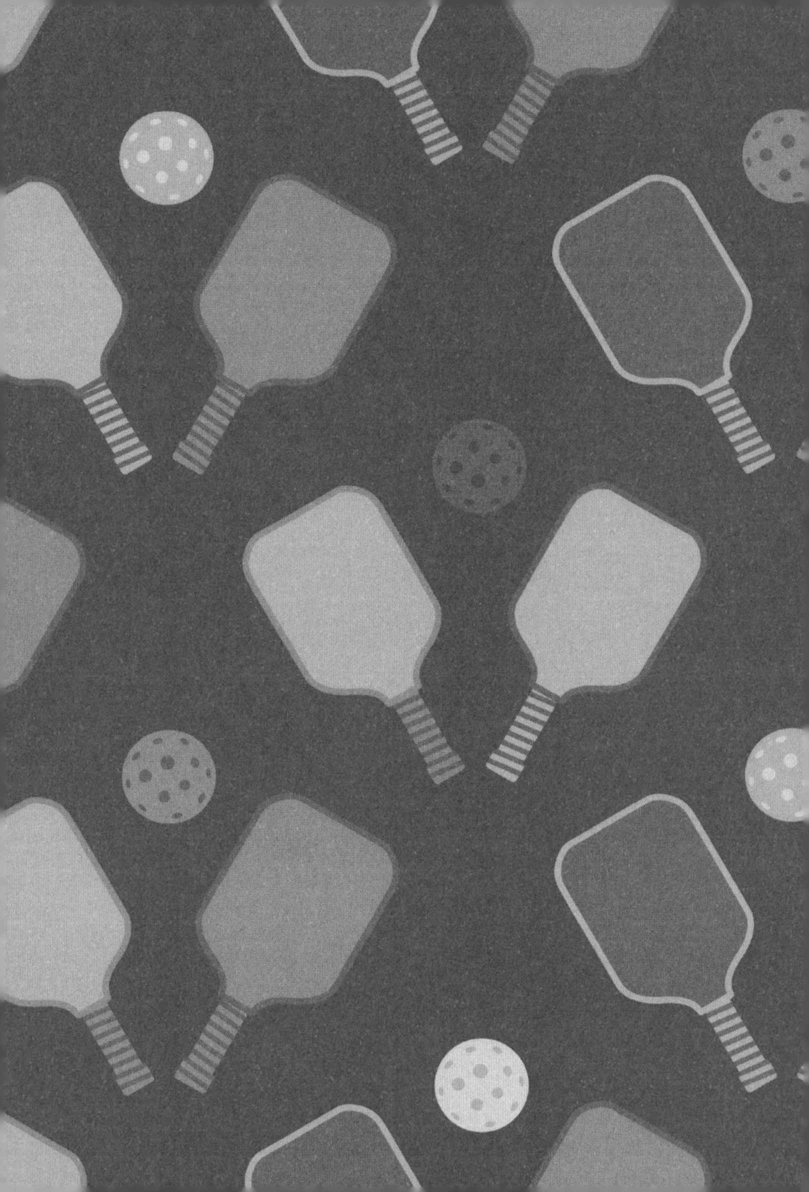

Chapter Two

Backyard Beginnings

A Congressman and a Businessman Walk into a Backyard...

The story of pickleball begins, somewhat surprisingly, in the summer of 1965. That's when Washington state congressman Joel Pritchard and businessman Bill Bell met for a round of golf. Afterwards, they went back to Pritchard's home on Bainbridge Island, just off the shores of Seattle, where their families were spending the weekend together.

But when they got back to Pritchard's place, they found their children bored and restless. Pritchard and Bell had to think fast and remembered a feature of the Bainbridge Island house that hadn't gotten much attention recently: the old badminton court.

Improvising a New Sport

Bell and Pritchard must have thought badminton would be the perfect way to entertain the group, but there was a slight problem: they didn't have enough badminton rackets for everyone to play.

What they *did* have were plenty of ping pong paddles, so they opted to try those instead. And rather than flinging a shuttlecock over the net like in a badminton match, the two decided their game would be played with a wiffle ball – a plastic sphere with holes in, usually used for a scaled-back baseball game.

What a Racket

Bell and Pritchard choosing ping pong paddles to play on the badminton court was a serendipitous decision, as it changed the trajectory of the game entirely. Let's compare their options.

Badminton racket typical dimensions:
26 in (67 cm) long, 8½–9 in (22–23 cm) wide.

A badminton racket is an open hoop with stretched strings, creating a bouncy "trampoline effect" which gives you extra lofty swings.

Ping pong paddle typical dimensions:
6¾ in (17 cm) long, 6 in (15 cm) wide.

Ping pong paddles are usually made of wood with a rubberized top-coat. With this denser racket, the idea is to bounce or even slam the ball over the net.

Adjusting the Net

With badminton in mind, Pritchard and Bell set up the rest of their new game. As such, they kept the net in the middle of the asphalt court at the badminton-official height of 5 ft (1.5 m).

But once the game began, the players realized something: their ping pong paddles were much better suited for making the perforated ball bounce on the asphalt, rather than volleying it over the net. To give the bounced ball a better chance of flying over the net, Pritchard and Bell lowered the net by roughly 2 ft (60 cm), and the game continued swimmingly.

"For me, joy + play = pickleball… The court might be the only place in the world where I'm fully in the now."

Brené Brown, Instagram, 29 October 2021

(Bestselling author Brené is the owner of ATX Pickleballers, a Major League Pickleball team.)

Weekend Warriors

In one weekend, Pritchard and Bell had a rough draft of what would become pickleball.

The next weekend, they brought another creator, Barney McCallum, to the island, and got to work nailing the rules of the game. Soon enough, they had the principles of their new sport, which drew many of its standards from badminton.

The most important thing to pickleball's creators was that their game could be played by people of all ages – it would be a family game, just the way it had started that weekend on Bainbridge Island.

The oldest registered pickleball player is 94 years old, while the youngest one is only 4 years old.

The First Official Pickleball Court

In 1967, the first official pickleball court was built in the garden of Bill O'Brian, one of Pritchard's friends and neighbours.

Now, there are more than 14,000 courts in the USA alone – an increase of 650 per cent in the last seven years!

Other countries are following suit: there are now 1,500 in Canada, 800 in Australia and 300 in the UK. Experts estimate that China will hit the 10,000 pickleball court mark by 2030.

“On the same court, you can have a millionaire with someone living pay check to pay check. No one’s interested in what you do for a living, only in how long you’ve been playing.”

Simone Jardim, pro pickleball player,
Vanity Fair, 21 October 2021

What's in a Name?

You've got to be wondering why in the world this game is called pickleball. It might even be why you bought this book.

Well, there are two solid theories, both of which are championed by different groups of people who were there when the sport was invented...

Theory #1
"Pickles has the ball!"

Once upon a time on Bainbridge Island, a family's dog had puppies, which they decided to give away for free to some of their neighbours. One of those puppies ended up with Joel Pritchard's family, who named the dog Pickles.

As the story goes, Pickles' family would play their new racket sport in the backyard, and Pickles got into the habit of chasing after the wiffle ball as it bounced back and forth over the net.

So, one weekend while the Pritchards were hanging out with two neighbouring families who also played the new sport, someone had a revelation: the game should be named after their four-legged friend who retrieved the ball.

Pickle(s)ball De-bunked?

Although many of the pickleball OGs stand by Pickles the dog as the inspiration for the sport's name, others say there's no way that's possible.

Why? Because, they say, Pickles the dog became part of the family *after* the sport already had its unique moniker. Both Pritchard's wife, Joan, and his daughter, Peggy, have negated this theory.

In fact, in 2008, Joan told her side of the story in a piece for a West Virginian newspaper.

> "Somehow the idea the name came from our dog Pickles was attached to the naming of the game, but Pickles wasn't on the scene for two more years. The dog was named for the game, but stories about the name's origin were funnier thinking the game was named for the dog."

Joan Pritchard, *Parkersburg News and Sentinel*, 27 July 2008

“The name of the game became pickleball after I said it reminded me of the pickle boat in crew where oarsmen were chosen from the leftovers of other boats.”

Joan Pritchard, *Parkersburg News and Sentinel*, 27 July 2008

Theory #2
A Pickle Boat

In the same article where she debunked the Pickles the dog story, Joan recalled how *she* remembered the naming of the sport her husband invented. And it was easy for her to do, because according to her, it was she who inspired the name “pickleball”.

Joan explained how she thought the new game – a rather thrown-together combination of ping pong paddles, a badminton net and a wiffle ball – had distinct parallels with another sport.

By 1972, pickleball had its official name.

In that year, the sport's founders started a corporation to protect their creation: Pickle Ball, Inc.

They also started selling paddles and pickleball kits as the sport took off (first, in the Pacific Northwest of the USA, and then in the snowbird states).

"Snowbird states"

There's no such thing as a snowbird in the avian sense, but they certainly exist in the geographical sense!

In the USA, snowbirds are people who live in places with cold winters – such as the Pacific Northwest – but travel south in search of warmer weather when temperatures start to dip.

In the case of pickleball, this meant the sport migrated from Washington state into places like Arizona, California, Hawaii and even Florida in a relatively short timeframe.

"I never thought I'd say this: as long as I can walk, I'm playing pickleball. I can't wait to get back on the court."

Andre Agassi, at the Pickleball Slam, ESPN, 2 April 2023

This was the year pickleball officially made it into all 50 American states – proof that it was, indeed, a sport for everyone, just as Pritchard and co. had hoped.

Chapter Three

Pickleball's Time to Shine

Pickleball Goes Global

The International Federation of Pickleball (IFP) was founded in 2010, with only four members:

- USA
- Canada
- India
- Spain

These countries banded together with the shared goal of promoting and developing pickleball the world over. (Spoiler alert: their efforts worked.)

Official statistics declared there were 36.5 million pickleball players in the USA in 2023.

Showing just how quickly the pickle star is rising, compare this to 8.9 million in 2022, and 3.3 million in 2018!

The average age of a pickleballer is 34.5, and the largest age bracket is 18–34, which makes up 28.8 per cent of all players.

Although it's sometimes thought of as a retirement sport, the stats don't lie!

80 Countries

In 2023, the IFP tweaked its name – it's now known as the International Pickleball Federation (IPF) – but its mission to stoke the growth and development of the sport remains.

There's one other *slight* difference – what used to have four member countries now has 80.

Going for Gold

The IPF has a worldwide audience, and an equally as global goal: they want to see pickleball added to the Olympic Games.

In 2024, Paris chose not to add pickleball in favour of other new sports (breakdancing, anyone?). And it won't feature at the Los Angeles 2028 games, either.

So, pickleball's next chance will be the 2032 Olympics in Brisbane, Australia. Come on the Aussies!

You might have already been aware that businessman and philanthropist Bill Gates is a keen pickler.

But what you probably don't know is that his father was friends with the guys who invented pickleball, meaning the Microsoft founder has played for a long time, and knows a lot more about the sport than the average player!

Top Tournaments

US Pickleball Open

Set in Naples, Florida, every year, this is the world's largest pickleball tournament. The 8th Annual US Open in April 2024 saw 35,000 spectators gather to watch 3,000 pickleballers going for the professional prize purse, a cool $100,000.

USA Pickleball National Championships

This tournament takes place each year in November. While the timing is set in stone, the location always changes – in 2024, players gathered in Mesa, Arizona, to compete for some serious prize money: $225,000.

The largest pickleball tournament outside of the USA – and the third largest contest overall – takes place in England.

In 2024, the English Open kicked off in Telford, Shropshire, with nearly 2,000 competitors hailing from 45 different countries and ranging from 8–80 years old!

One of the most exciting moments of the week-long event? Underdog Mollie Knaggs won the Women's Pro Singles competition in her home country, delighting fans who gathered to watch the final match.

Opening Up

From 2025 the Professional Pickleball Association (PPA) Tour and Major League Pickleball are partnering up to take their tournaments global. Catch your favourite players at…

- **The Australia Pickleball Open:** Melbourne – January
- **The India Pickleball Open:** Mumbai – February
- **The Canada Pickleball Open:** Toronto – September
- **The Asia Pickleball Open:** October
- **The Europe Pickleball Open:** October

In a short video she posted to promote her 2024 album, *The Tortured Poets Department*, Taylor Swift spliced together snippets of her life behind the scenes. Eagle-eyed fans noticed she was holding a pickleball paddle in one of the clips.

US Leagues

The top three leagues in the USA are:

- **Major League Pickleball (MLP)**
- **Professional Pickleball Association (PPA)**
- **Association of Pickleball Players (APP)**

The total prize money for the events held by these leagues is estimated to be between **$9–11 million**.

Major League Pickleball began in 2021 in the USA and includes 24 teams.

A dozen of them are in the Premier Level, while the other 12 play at the Challenger Level. Teams can go up and down the levels like they do in Premier League soccer.

Pickleball's Best & Brightest #1

Ben Johns

Ben Johns hails from Laytonsville, Maryland, and currently resides in Austin, Texas. He is the No. 1 male pickleball player in the world – and is considered to be the greatest pickleball player of all time.

Ben was the 2023 PPA Tournament Finals champion in men's singles, men's doubles, *and* in mixed doubles. But that's not even close to being his most impressive accolade.

His highlights include:

- **A 108-match winning streak in singles**
- **123 PPA titles (as of 2024)**
- **21 Triple Crowns, meaning he won the singles, doubles and mixed doubles in the same tournament**

Former talk-show host Ellen DeGeneres loves pickleball so much that she has designed some of her own paddles, which she's sold to benefit her charity, The Ellen Fund.

While on a break from filming, Oscar winner Leonardo DiCaprio noticed some people playing pickleball and decided to try it out for himself. Nowadays, he's a seasoned pickler, and is even known for organizing charity matches.

Pickleball's Best & Brightest #2

Collin Johns

There's something in the Johns family genes, because there's not just one star pickleball player in their midst – but two.

Collin is Ben Johns' older brother, and partially credits his success to training he received from his younger sibling. (He also attributes it to playing baseball, tennis and table tennis.)

Together, the Johns brothers have won more than 25 professional titles as doubles partners.

Collin has quite an impressive singles career as well – he has won 31 titles.

Pickleball's Best & Brightest #3

Anna Leigh Waters

According to the PPA, Anna Leigh Waters is "pickleball's biggest star". Born in 2007, her pro journey started when she was just 12 years old!

Anna Leigh discovered pickleball at her grandfather's house, and from there, she started playing doubles with her mother as her partner.

The duo pioneered a new style of pickleball by the time they went pro. Instead of the passive style of play that so many players stuck to, waiting for their opponents to fault to get service back, the Waters played by "banging" and "ripping" the ball aggressively to get on top of the leaderboard.

Nowadays, Anna Leigh is still a teenager, and also still at the top of her game. In 2024, she was the highest-paid pickleball player, with projected earnings of more than $3 million (£2.3 million)!

Leading pro players are estimated to earn $100,000–250,000 (£77,000–190,000) annually from a combination of prize money, endorsements, coaching and other sources.

(Anna Leigh Waters' million-dollar earnings are not the norm!)

Pickleball's Best & Brightest #4

Simone Jardim

Simone Jardim retired from professional pickleball in 2022, but was ranked as the No. 1 women's player in the world from 2016–2020. She was called the "queen of pickleball" by many, and she certainly earned her crown!

Simone won four consecutive singles titles in the US Open Pickleball Championships, including two Triple Crown wins for singles, doubles and mixed doubles in 2017 and 2018. (She used to play mixed doubles with Ben Johns!) In total, she earned 32 PPA titles throughout her career.

Jardim was best known for her unique "ready" position, excellent footwork and quick reflexes. Her backhand was one of the best in the game, and her ability to mix up shots made her a tough opponent to beat.

Pickleball's Best & Brightest #5

Tyson McGuffin

Tyson McGuffin was a seasoned tennis player and coach who decided to dabble in pickleball – but it didn't go well for him at first. Unlike so many of his tennis-playing peers, pickleball did *not* come easy to Tyson. But he kept at it, and within half a year, he became a pro pickleballer in 2016.

Since then, Tyson has become a fan-favourite pickler for his skill and personality. He's also extremely involved in the proliferation of pickleball nationwide. He helms instructional videos, runs pickleball clinics and does anything else he can to get more people on the court.

How to Become a Pro Pickler

It takes a lot of work to go pro, but it's not *impossible*. Here's some of the best advice to get you playing with the big guns:

1. Hire a coach

Many coaches have played professionally themselves so they will have the best pointers for sharpening your game and going pro.

2. Practise – a *lot*

You'll need to practise and train about 5–6 days a week.

3. Boost your fitness levels

Pro pickleballers do all kinds of cross-training, including cycling, yoga and swimming, as well as weightlifting to strengthen both the upper and lower body.

4. Sign up for amateur tournaments
Amateur tournaments are a great way to tap into your competitive side. Tournament play will also give you points that will boost your ranking, which will help you in your efforts to become a pro.

5. Join a league
Joining a professional pickleball league will give you access to higher-stakes tournaments. Plus, it will help you connect with pros, coaches and other powerful picklers.

6. Go after the golden ticket
Every year at the National Pickleball Tournament, amateur pickleballers have the chance to compete with the pros. All you have to do is win one of the 17 or so Golden Ticket Tournaments held across the country in the year before the main event. If you want to play in the big leagues, securing this wild card may be your quickest path to the top!

Tennis Pros Love Pickleball

The transition from tennis to pickleball court is a popular one, and some of the racket sport's greatest players are now keen pickleballers.

Serena Williams

Yes, the GOAT has picked up a paddle – Williams is an avid participant. She first took up pickleball as a way to vary her tennis training, but quickly fell in love with the game and plays it in tandem with the sport that made her a star.

Andre Agassi

Agassi won eight Grand Slam singles titles, along with an Olympic gold medal. But his love for racket sports didn't end when he retired from tennis in 2006. Nowadays, Agassi is a well-known pickleball player. He's often seen playing against other celebs – and he even signs up for pickleball tournaments just for fun sometimes!

John McEnroe

When McEnroe said, "By the way, pickleball sucks", in 2022, it seemed like he'd never become a pickler. But just a year later, he told *Forbes*, "My buddies like to play [pickleball] with me and it's an equalizer, so that was how I started playing originally." He's also been spotted on the court with retired NFL quarterback Drew Brees.

Andy Roddick

Roddick also rejected the idea of playing pickleball at first… until he got invited to take part in the first-ever Pickleball Slam exhibition, where the prize purse was a whopping $1 million (£770,000). He competed alongside Andre Agassi in the doubles competition, winning the massive prize over none other than McEnroe and his teammate, Michael Chang.

"I love pickleball. Isn't it fun? And I love that it's everywhere now. It could be a second career of mine, too."

Serena Williams, on *The Ellen DeGeneres Show*, 2 May 2022

Pickleball's Best & Brightest #6

Federico Staksrud

A common theme among the world's best pickleball players is that they began their career as tennis players, only to eventually find their way to the pickleball court. Federico Staksrud falls into this category.

The Buenos Aires native played competitive collegiate tennis at numerous schools, including the University of New Orleans and Tennessee Wesleyan University. However, it wasn't until he transferred to Florida Gulf Coast University for his master's degree in Information Systems that he dabbled in pickleball.

Fortunately for Staksrud, he had a team full of pickleball pros ready to guide him, including one of the greatest female players of all time, Simone Jardim. Although Staksrud has only played for two years, his ascension to the No. 2 ranking proves he could be on the brink of catching the immortal Johns.

Pop Culture Picklers

Brian Griffin is a fictional dog from the animated television series *Family Guy*. He's highly intellectual and well-read, and he's the voice of reason in the Griffin family.

In season 16, episode 5, Brian plays a game of pickleball against his opponent Gene Porterfield. Porterfield wins the match, but Brian, being the smart hound that he is, files a grievance against Gene for wearing marking shoes on the court – in real life, this is not allowed on many pickleball courts, either! Porterfield gets kicked out, and Brian becomes the pickleball consolation ladder champion.

Part of the Team

Celebrities don't just play the game – they invest in it, too!

These A-listers have put funds into teams in the Major League Pickleball (MLP):

- Brené Brown (author)
- Drake (rapper)
- Draymond Green (basketball player)
- Drew Brees (former American football player)
- Kevin Durant (basketball player)
- Kevin Love (basketball player)
- LeBron James (basketball player)
- Michael B. Jordan (actor)
- Tom Brady (former American football player)

"We're going to keep bringing awareness to this thing all around the country, all around the world. [...] I love that's it's become such a popular neighbourhood sport. It's a great way to get out of the house, but I'm coming to win. I'm coming to the dominate the sport."

Tom Brady, Instagram, October 2022

Pop star Katy Perry loves pickleball so much that she hosted a celebrity pickleball tournament in 2024 to benefit her charity, the Firework Foundation.

Participants included Orlando Bloom, Charlie Puth, Rob Lowe and Ellen DeGeneres.

Chapter Four

The A–Z of Pickleball

"There is nothing bad about this sport. It's social. It's friendly. It's competitive. It's a heck of a workout. When you find it, you don't leave it – and you go tell your friends about it."

Terri Graham, co-founder of the
US Open Pickleball Championships,
Naples Daily News, 24 April 2022

Here you'll find some of the most common pickleball terms – a pickle-tionary, if you will.

You may have heard some of these words – remember, the game's creators did pull inspiration from other sports – but there are some that are nearly as unique as the name "pickleball" itself.

A

Ace: A serve that is not returned by the opposing player/team, winning the serving player/team an instant point.

Around the post (ATP): Rather than travelling over the net, this shot reaches the other team's territory by going around the net post. This is usually possible when a ball bounces toward the edge of the court, at an outwards angle. Before the ball hits the floor again (and is out), the returner runs wide, and, with an unobstructed view (no post or net in the way), hits the ball straight into the other side of the court.

B

Backcourt: The area behind the kitchen.

Baseline: The back boundary of the pickleball court, which runs parallel to and is 22 ft (6.7 m) away from the net.

Backhand: Hitting the ball on your non-dominant side. How can you tell it's your non-dominant side? The back of your hand will be facing toward the net.

Backspin: When you move your paddle from a high to low position as you strike the ball, it changes its spinning direction. This means the ball will likely take a different trajectory over the net than expected, which can trip up an opponent.

Banger: A nickname for a pickleball player who likes to strike the ball VERY hard in an opponent's direction, making it difficult for them to return it.

Carry: Usually, the pickleball bounces right off the paddle, but if it glides along the face of the paddle through a forward hit, this is called a carry.

Cross-court: The side of the court diagonally across from where you're standing.

D

Dead ball: A ball that is no longer in play due to a fault.

Dig: A defensive shot to take when a ball is hit low toward you, near your feet. By crouching low and absorbing the power of the offensive shot, you can dig the ball and pop it back over the net.

Dink: A controlled, slow shot taken from just behind the non-volley zone line and designed to land in the opposing team/player's kitchen, where they can't volley it back. Dinks are a great way to slow down the pace of the game – it's a strategic shot you should practise and have in your arsenal!

Double hit: A rare situation in which a single, continuous swing results in a player's paddle hitting the ball twice. This is the only situation where a double hit is allowed in pickleball!

Drive: A powerful forehand shot, typically made from the backcourt or mid-court, that travels straight and low.

Drop shot: Similar to a dink but made from anywhere on the court (usually toward the baseline), this gentle shot is designed to land in the kitchen, where opponents can't return it with an attacking shot.

E

Erne: A volley shot taken from either the back left or right boundary of the kitchen, named after its inventor, pickleball player Erne Perry.

In an interview with the PPA Tour in 2023 Perry explained that the term sprung from a game at the 2010 National Pickleball Championships: “We were playing a team that liked to hit the ball straight across the net and I did that ‘Erne’ shot to them repeatedly in the game, and some of the people that were watching ended up calling it the Erne because I did it so many times”.

F

Face: The part of the pickleball paddle that hits the ball.

Falafel: A shot you don't want to make! A falafel happens when you hit the pickleball with little-to-no power, so it falls short of making it over the net.

Fault: An error or mistake. If made by an opposing player, you get a point. If the serving player faults, service changes.

Flamingo: You'll be able to picture how this one looks – it's a shot taken in a flamingo-like pose, standing on one leg and leaning forward to hit the ball. Players deploy flamingo shots when they're in need of a powerful, attacking shot.

Follow-through: The part of a pickleball shot that occurs after the pickleball has made contact with the paddle. Your follow-through helps chart the ball's trajectory over the net.

Forehand: A shot made when you swing with your hand facing forward, a much more dominant shot than the backhand!

G

Getting pickled/the golden pickle: A very nice way of saying that one of the two players/teams in a match scores no points by the end of the game.

Ground stroke: When the ball is hit after a single bounce.

Half-volley: When a ball is hit just after it bounces, so it does not have the chance to reach its full height.

Kitchen: Also known as the non-volley zone, this is the 7-ft (2.1 m) space that stretches from the net to mid-court on either side. In this area, players cannot hit the pickleball unless it bounces first.

Let: It used to be that when a ball clipped the net and landed in the playable area cross-court (a let ball) it was considered not in play; however now, gameplay continues and the serve is good.

Line call: In a game with a referee, a line call will be made when the ball has gone out of bounds.

Lob: A high and far-reaching shot designed to push players back to return from nearer to the baseline; however, it can also allow the receiving team to make a powerful shot if they reach the ball in time.

M

Mid-court: The area that sits between the kitchen and the baseline; also known as the transition zone or no-man's land.

N

Nasty Nelson: A strategic shot to take if the opposing team isn't paying attention, this one's literally aimed at the receiving player closest to the net – if it hits them, they commit a fault, and the serving team gets a point.

O

Open paddle face: Turning your paddle to a 45-degree angle (facing the net) – this positioning is key to executing the dink shot.

P

Paddle tap: The sportsmanlike way to end a pickleball match – players tap the bottom of their paddle to their opponent's.

Paddy: A slang name for your paddle.

Painting the line: A well-executed shot that looks like it's going out of bounds, but lands just inside the court.

Pickler: Someone who loves playing pickleball.

Poach: If you're playing doubles and cross the court to hit a ball moving toward your partner, you've poached the shot.

R

Rally: The continuous play that happens after a serve, until a fault stops the back and forth.

Receiver: The player standing diagonally opposite to the server, who returns the serve.

S

Sidelines: The left- and right-hand boundaries of the court.

Side-out: When one player/team loses service and it's transferred to the other side.

Skinny singles: A way of playing singles where the court is cut in half, therefore reducing the ground that players have to cover.

Smash: A powerful overhead shot.

Stacking: A doubles strategy in which both players stand on the same side of the court during the serve, then quickly transition to their respective sides after the pickleball is returned.

T

Tweener: A ball hit between the legs, either because a ball is hit at an awkward angle and that's the only option, or to show off!

U

Unforced error: When a pickleball player makes a mistake and faults all on their own – no strategy from the opposing team required.

V

Volley: When a player hits the ball in the air before it bounces – this is not allowed in the kitchen.

Y

Yips: A player is said to have the yips if they repeatedly miss serving the ball into the correct spot on the court.

"You've got to be able to hit the ball hard. Nobody plays golf to putt."

Joel Pritchard, pickleball's co-inventor, *An Oral History*, Washington State Legislature, 2000